JAPAN

Tom Streissguth

Lerner Publications Company • Minneapolis

The editor wishes to thank Harumi Terabayashi and Paul Hahn for their assistance with this book.

Lerner Publications Company
A division of Lerner Publishing Group, Inc.
241 First Avenue North
Minneapolis, MN 55401 U.S.A.

Website address: www.lernerbooks.com

Library of Congress Cataloging-in-Publication Data

Streissguth, Thomas, 1958–
    Japan / by Tom Streissguth.
      p. cm. — (Country explorers)
    Includes index.
    ISBN 978–0–8225–8659–3 (lib. bdg. : alk. paper)
    1. Japan—Juvenile literature. I. Title.
    DS806.S77 2008
    952—dc22   2007024879

Manufactured in the United States of America
1 2 3 4 5 6 – PA – 13 12 11 10 09 08

Table of Contents

Welcome!

Water, water everywhere. Japan is a country made up of four thousand islands. Islands are pieces of land with water on all sides. The great Pacific Ocean washes against eastern Japan. To the west lies the Sea of Japan. The big piece of land on the other side of the sea is the continent of Asia.

This town on Honshu Island is near the Pacific Ocean and Mount Fuji.

4

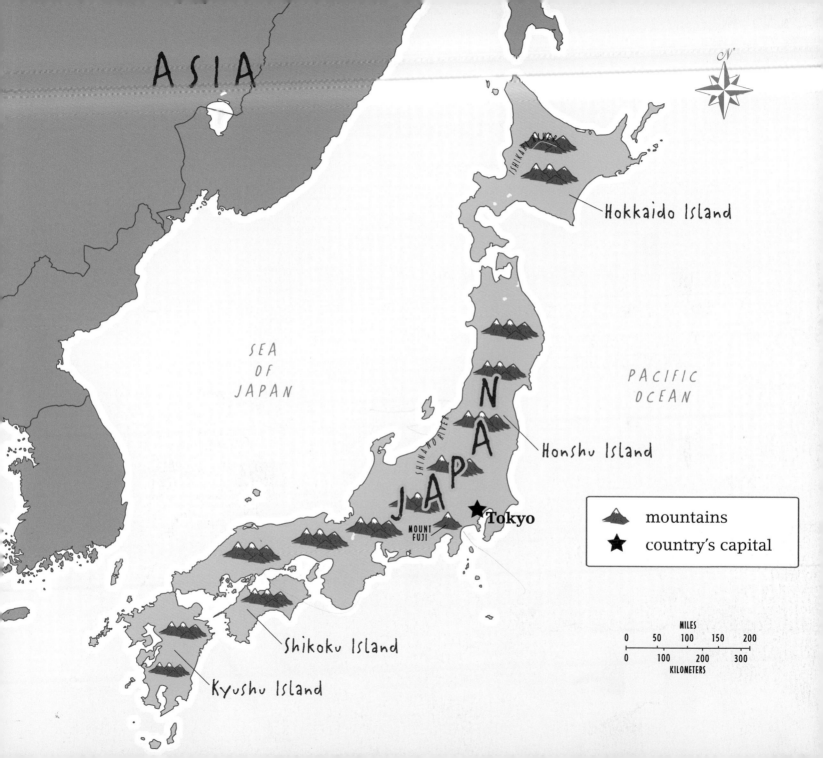

ASIA

SEA
OF
JAPAN

PACIFIC
OCEAN

ISHIKARI RIVER

Hokkaido Island

SHINANO RIVER

N

Honshu Island

J A P A N

★ **Tokyo**

MOUNT
FUJI

Shikoku Island

Kyushu Island

⛰	mountains
★	country's capital

MILES
0   50   100   150   200

0   100   200   300
KILOMETERS

Crowded Country

Where do people in Japan live? Mountains cover much of Japan's land. So most people live in the few places where the land is flat.

Japan's biggest cities are along the coast.

Japanese cities are crowded—especially Tokyo. Workers and shoppers fill the sidewalks. Giant traffic jams stop cars and trucks on the streets. Underground, people pack into trains called subways.

Bullet Train

Faster than a bus! A car! A speeding bullet?! Well, not quite. Bullet trains take people from city to city in Japan. At nearly 186 miles (300 kilometers) per hour, they'll get there fast!

Businessmen line up to take a bullet train from Tokyo to Kyushu Island.

Volcanoes

The mountains of Japan are actually old volcanoes. A volcano is a hole in the ground where melted rock can flow out. Some volcanoes spit, gurgle, and smoke. Others have been quiet for many years. Japan's most famous volcano is Mount Fuji.

Smoke billows out of Mount Asama. It is one of the biggest and most active volcanoes in Japan.

These people are relaxing in a hot spring.

A Hot Bath

The inside of Earth is very hot. Hot rock heats up water that lies underground. In some spots, the heated water comes out through a crack in the ground. A pool of water called a hot spring forms. The Japanese like to visit these springs to take a long, hot soak.

People look through what is left of their homes after a powerful earthquake shook northern Japan.

Danger!

An earthquake is felt somewhere in Japan every day! Most of the earthquakes are small. The ground begins to rumble and shake. Then, everything is still. Big earthquakes can cause buildings to fall down. The Japanese make buildings that move with the ground so they don't fall down as easily.

Giant waves called tsunamis can be a danger on the coast. An earthquake on the seafloor can cause these huge waves. The walls of water are sometimes as tall as a house.

The Giant Catfish

One Japanese folktale says that a giant catfish lives beneath the land. Once in a while, the catfish swings its huge tail and starts another *jishin*—or earthquake.

Japanese schoolchildren are taught to take cover if an earthquake hits.

First People

Ancestors of the Ainu were some of the first people to live on the Japanese islands. The Ainu still live on Hokkaido. Can you find the island of Hokkaido on the map on page 5?

An Ainu man makes a wooden carving.

12

Ainu gather for the festival of Marimo Matsuri. It is held to honor and protect a water plant that grows in lakes.

Some Ainu practice their old ways of life. They fish and grow rice. The younger Ainu go to Japanese schools and work in Japanese cities. The old Ainu ways are mixing with Japanese ways to make new traditions.

13

The Japanese

Many years ago, Japan's leaders closed off the country to the rest of the world. They didn't want strangers from other countries to change Japan. No one could enter or leave Japan. Because of this, most Japanese people share the same language and culture.

Japanese teenagers like to make up styles of their own.

Cooperation is a big part of Japanese culture. Japanese people feel it is important to work together. That goes for people in a family, in a school, in a business, or as a country.

Students bow to their teachers in a Japanese classroom. When a Japanese person bows, it is polite to bow back.

Newcomers

Nowadays, Japan welcomes many visitors and ideas from outside Japan. Japanese culture, ideas, and people have traveled the world too.

Three boys study a model car at a Honda factory. Cars designed in Japan are popular all over the world.

Japanese kids learn some soccer tips from an Italian player.

People from other countries also live in Japan. They come from places such as Korea, China, the Philippines, Brazil, Peru, and the United States. Some immigrants come to work. Others come to raise families.

The Family

In Japan, most families are made up of a mother, a father, and one or two children. Some children live with just one parent. In other families, grandparents live with their children and grandchildren.

A Japanese family sits down for a meal.

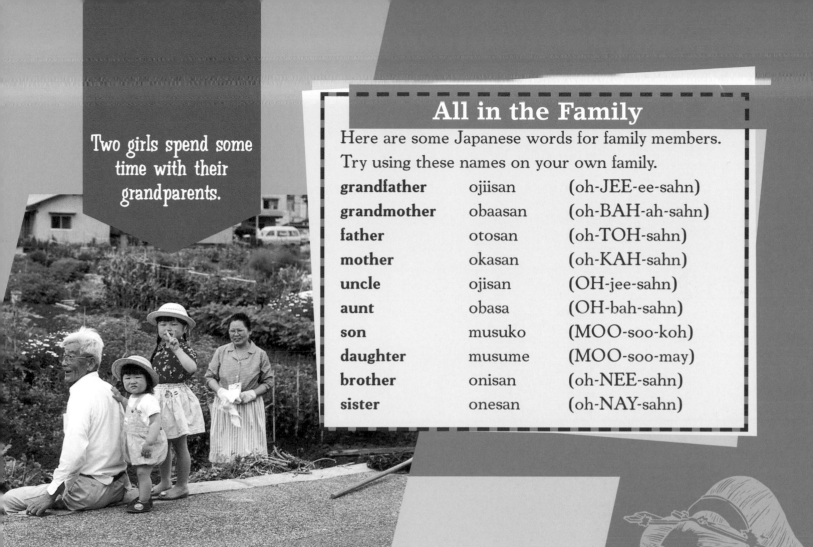

Two girls spend some time with their grandparents.

All in the Family

Here are some Japanese words for family members. Try using these names on your own family.

grandfather	ojiisan	(oh-JEE-ee-sahn)
grandmother	obaasan	(oh-BAH-ah-sahn)
father	otosan	(oh-TOH-sahn)
mother	okasan	(oh-KAH-sahn)
uncle	ojisan	(OH-jee-sahn)
aunt	obasa	(OH-bah-sahn)
son	musuko	(MOO-soo-koh)
daughter	musume	(MOO-soo-may)
brother	onisan	(oh-NEE-sahn)
sister	onesan	(oh-NAY-sahn)

In many Japanese families, the father has an office job and the mother works at home. The parent who stays at home makes the meals and takes care of the children. She or he also handles the family's money.

19

The Home

In big cities in Japan, most homes are small. Many people live in high-rise apartments. A family may share a tiny kitchen, a living room, and one or two small bedrooms.

High-rise buildings like these take up less land than houses.

Country homes are larger. Older houses have few walls inside. The Japanese use sliding paper screens to build walls wherever they want. That way a room can be made bigger or smaller.

Tatami

In Japan, straw mats called tatami cover the floors in a house. To keep the mats clean, the Japanese take off their shoes.

Tatami mats cover the floor of this room. Can you guess where people sit?

School

It's a warm spring day in April. Do you know what that means? The new school year has just begun in Japan. Japanese children start school when they are six years old. They spend most of the day at school.

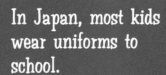

In Japan, most kids wear uniforms to school.

22

At the end of the day, students clean their classrooms and hallways. In the afternoons, they may go to an after-school activity. Then they go home. After dinner, it's time to do homework. In Japan, doing well in school is very important.

Counting in Japanese

Here is some homework for you. Try counting from one to ten in Japanese.

1	ichi	(EE-chee)
2	ni	(NEE)
3	san	(SAHN)
4	shi	(SHEE)
5	go	(GOH)
6	roku	(ROH-koo)
7	shichi	(SHEE-chee)
8	hachi	(HAH-chee)
9	ku	(KOO)
10	ju	(JOO)

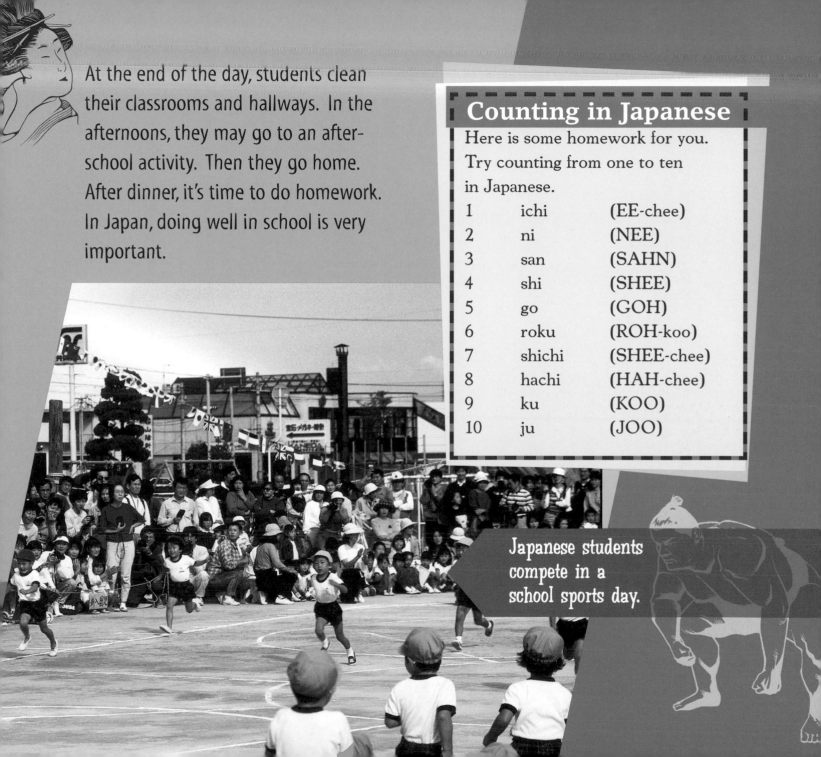

Japanese students compete in a school sports day.

Food

The most important food to the Japanese is rice. They grow it everywhere. *Gohan*, the word for meal, actually has two meanings. It means "cooked rice" too.

A woman plants rice by hand in northern Japan.

Click, Click, Click

The Japanese eat with two wooden sticks called *hashi*. They are chopsticks. Do you know how to use chopsticks?

This is a bento box.

For lunch, a Japanese person might bring a *bento*. This lunch comes in a small box. Inside is rice or noodles. Rice balls wrapped with seaweed are popular too. A bento box may also hold fish, meat, tofu, or eggs. And there is always room for tasty vegetables and fruits. What would you pack in your bento?

Religion

The oldest religion in Japan is Shinto. Followers of Shinto
believe that all natural things have spirits. Volcanoes,
mountains, trees, and rocks all have spirits. To pray to the
spirits, people visit a *jinja*. People pray for many things, such
as good luck in school or for a successful crop.

Buddhism came to Japan from other parts of Asia. Buddhists believe that happiness comes from the way a person lives. It does not come from money or things, such as toys or a big house.

Two people stand in front of a giant statue of Buddha in Japan. Buddha's teachings became the Buddhist religion.

27

Holidays

Happy New Year! The biggest holiday in Japan takes place in January. Schools and stores close. Families clean and decorate their homes. They pray at jinjas and Buddhist temples.

Firefighters balance on ladders during their New Year's parade in Tokyo.

28

Colorful wind socks shaped like carp fly in the breeze on Children's Day.

These young children are dressed as Japan's royal court for the Festival of Dolls.

In Japan, boys and girls each have their own holiday. The girls celebrate the Festival of Dolls on March 3. Families set fancy dolls on shelves for everyone to see. Boys celebrate Children's Day on May 5. Families fly a wind sock shaped like a carp for each son. They hope their sons will be as healthy as this big, strong fish.

Playtime

Where does your family go for vacations? Japanese people enjoy taking a trip to the ocean in the summer. In the winter, they can go skiing in the mountains.

Sunbathers and swimmers spend a day at the beach in southwest Japan.

A man and two boys try out video games at a store in Tokyo.

On most weekends, Japanese families visit relatives in the country, explore parks, or go shopping. Of course, many Japanese kids think that playing video games is far more fun.

Everyone, Sing!

Karaoke is another way Japanese people pass time. A machine plays recorded music. The words to the song appear on a screen. Someone from the audience sings along.

Sports

The Japanese are crazy about *yakyu*, or baseball. The rules are the same as they are in American baseball. But the ballpark is different. It is smaller in Japan because land is hard to come by. Soccer has many fans too.

Japan's Naoki Miyanishi gets ready to throw a pitch.

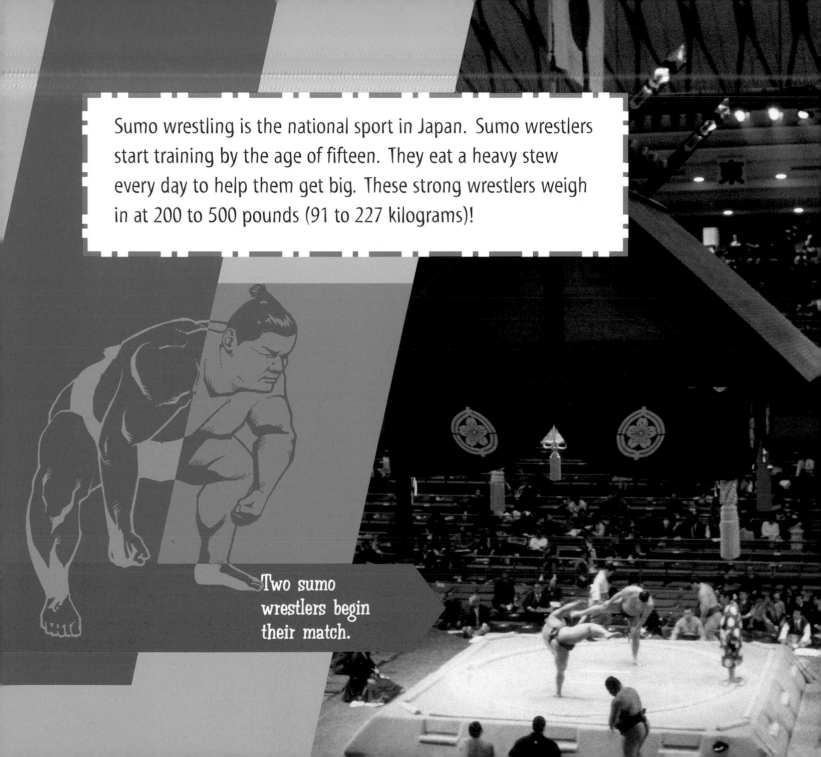

Sumo wrestling is the national sport in Japan. Sumo wrestlers start training by the age of fifteen. They eat a heavy stew every day to help them get big. These strong wrestlers weigh in at 200 to 500 pounds (91 to 227 kilograms)!

Two sumo wrestlers begin their match.

Martial Arts

Martial arts are more than just kicks and punches. Judo, aikido, kendo, and karate teach people how to protect themselves and how to fight back. Students also learn to control their body and mind in a fight. Each martial art has special moves. Some students practice for years.

Aikido uses twists, holds, and throws.

Dear Mom and Dad,

Konnichiwa! (That means "hello" in Japanese.) I'm having a great time studying in Japan. Every day after classes, we go to a special school where we learn kendo. We use bamboo swords and wear metal masks, gloves, and cool body armor. The fighters try to touch the other person's head, chest, wrists, and throats. I'm not very good yet, but I sure am having fun!

See you soon!

Your

Any

Anywhe

JAPAN

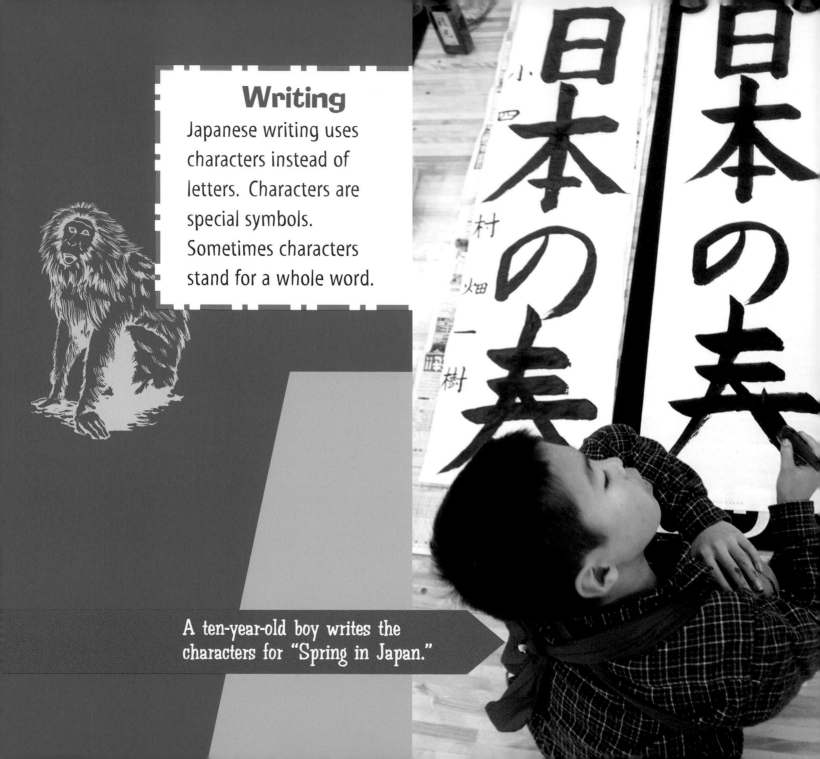

Writing

Japanese writing uses characters instead of letters. Characters are special symbols. Sometimes characters stand for a whole word.

A ten-year-old boy writes the characters for "Spring in Japan."

Other times, characters stand for part of a word or for a word sound. Here's an example. The word for *soccer* in Japanese is *sakkaa.* It is written as four characters. They stand for the sounds of the English word.

These street signs show the different kinds of Japanese characters.

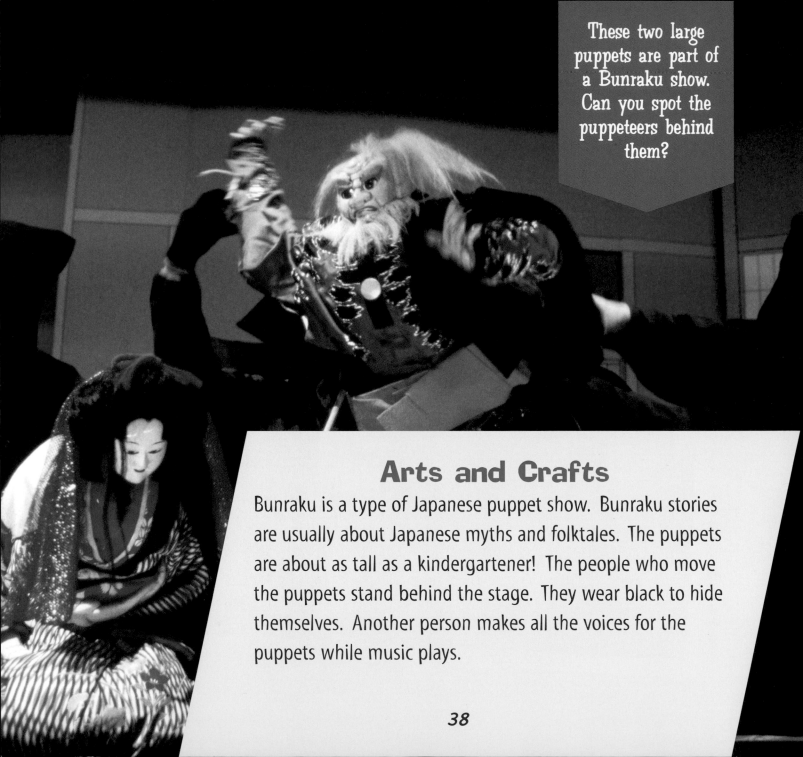

These two large puppets are part of a Bunraku show. Can you spot the puppeteers behind them?

Arts and Crafts

Bunraku is a type of Japanese puppet show. Bunraku stories are usually about Japanese myths and folktales. The puppets are about as tall as a kindergartener! The people who move the puppets stand behind the stage. They wear black to hide themselves. Another person makes all the voices for the puppets while music plays.

Origami

Can you imagine turning a flat piece of paper into a lion or a bird? This is called origami. Origami is Japanese for "fold paper." Designs for origami can be simple or hard.

Origami is a form of art. People fold pieces of paper into beautiful shapes.

Japanese Comics

If you like comic books, you'll like Japanese manga. The Japanese are famous for these comic-book drawings. Some manga are about superheroes fighting evil. The story keeps going each week or month. Other manga tell stories of love, sports, or mystery.

Kids and adults who like to read manga have many choices.

Some manga characters and stories are made into TV shows and movies. Manga artists use computers to make moving cartoons called anime. Anime is packed with color, sound, and action.

A model poses next to Goku. He is the hero of the manga and anime series Dragon Ball Z.

Music

The place to go for every kind of music in Japan is Shibuya. Shibuya is a section of Tokyo. You can find people playing jazz music, rock music, and folk music all in the same neighborhood.

A musician plays for a group of teenagers in Tokyo.

A Loyal Dog

In Shibuya stands the statue of a loyal dog named Hachiko. Hachiko waited for his master in the same spot every night. He did not know that his master had died. The statue has become a popular meeting place for friends.

This street in Shibuya is a popular place for young Japanese to meet, shop, and hang out.

43

THE FLAG OF JAPAN

The flag of Japan is named Hinomaru. It became the official flag in 1870. Hinomaru is a red circle in the middle of a white box. The red circle stands for the rising sun. The Japanese call their country Nihon or Nippon. It means "where the sun comes from."

FAST FACTS

FULL COUNTRY NAME: Nihon (or Nippon) Koku (Land of the Rising Sun)

AREA: 145,869 square miles (377,801 square kilometers), slightly less than the size of Montana

MAIN LANDFORMS: main islands of Honshu, Hokkaido, Kyushu, Shikoku; the island chain Ryukyu; the mountain range Japanese Alps; the volcanoes Mount Fuji and Mount Asama; the plains Kanto and Osaka

MAJOR RIVERS: Ishikari, Shinano

ANIMALS AND THEIR HABITATS: Japanese macaques, or snow monkeys (mountains, forests); brown bears, red foxes, Amami rabbits (forests); cranes, herons, giant salamanders (rivers and ponds)

CAPITAL CITY: Tokyo

OFFICIAL LANGUAGE: Japanese

POPULATION: about 127,800,000

GLOSSARY

ancestors: relatives who lived long ago

character: a picture or symbol that stands for a whole word or word sound

continent: any one of seven large areas of land. The continents are Africa, Antarctica, Asia, Australia, Europe, North America, and South America.

earthquake: a shaking of the ground caused by shifting underground rock

folktale: a timeless story told by word of mouth from grandparent to parent to child. Many folktales have been written down in books.

hot spring: heated water from underground that makes its way through a crack in Earth's surface and forms a pool above ground

immigrants: people who move from a home country to another country to live

island: a piece of land surrounded by water

martial art: one of several ways of fighting and protecting oneself. Martial arts include judo, kendo, aikido, and karate.

subway: an underground train that takes people to spots within a city

tradition: a way of doing things—such as preparing a meal, celebrating a holiday, or making a living—that a group of people have practiced for a long time

volcano: an opening in Earth's surface through which hot, melted rock shoots up

TO LEARN MORE

BOOKS

Dean, Arlan. *Samurai: Warlords of Japan.* New York: Children's Press, 2005. Learn about the Samurai, mighty Japanese warriors.

Lattimore, Deborah Nourse. *The Fool and the Phoenix: A Tale of Ancient Japan.* New York: Joanna Cotler Books, 1997. Follow the adventures of Hideo the fool as he falls in love with a beautiful fairy.

Littlefield, Holly. *Colors of Japan.* Minneapolis: Millbrook Press, 1997. Discover Japan through this warmly illustrated introduction to the Land of the Rising Sun.

Poisson, Barbara Aoki. *The Ainu of Japan.* Minneapolis: Lerner Publications Company, 2002. Read more about the Ainu, first people of Japan.

Reynolds, Jeff. *Japan.* New York: Children's Press, 2005. Experience Japan from A to Z.

WEBSITES

Japan
http://www.timeforkids.com/TFK/hh/go places/main/0,20344,555016,00.html This website from the magazine *Time for Kids* features virtual tours of Japan, a language page, a quiz, and more.

Kids Web Japan
http://web-japan.org/kidsweb/ Explore Japan with legends, quizzes, fun games, and tons of facts.

INDEX

The photographs in this book are used with the permission of: © DAJ/Getty Images, pp. 4, 20; © age fotostock/SuperStock, pp. 6, 26, 35, 40; © Kazuhiro Nogi/AFP/Getty Images, pp. 7, 17, 29 (left); © Koichi Kamoshida/Getty Images, p. 8; Photo by Paul J. Buklarewicz, pp. 9, 19, 23, 33; AP Photo/Koji Sasahara, p. 10; AP Photo/Kyodo News, p. 11; © David Kleyn/Alamy, p. 12; © Gavin Hellier/Robert Harding World Imagery/Corbis, p. 13; © Peter Horree/Alamy, p. 14; © christian kober/Alamy, p. 15; © Yoshikazu Tsuno/AFP/Getty Images, pp. 16, 29 (right); © Chad Ehlers/Alamy, p. 18; © Misha Gordon/Alamy, p. 21; © Kiriko Shirobayashi/Stone/Getty Images, p. 22; © Robert Harding Picture Library Ltd/Alamy, p. 24; © Cephas Picture Library/Alamy, p. 25; © Olivier Martel/Corbis, p. 27; © Toshiki Sawaguchi/epa/Corbis, p. 28; © Toshitaka Morita/Sebun Photo/Getty Images, p. 30; AP Photo/Shizuo Kambayashi, p. 31; © Khaled Desouki/AFP/Getty Images, p. 32; © Roberto Pastrovicchio/Alamy, p. 34; © Reuters/CORBIS, p. 36; © Tohoku Color Agency/Japan Images/Getty Images, p. 37; © Michael S. Yamashita/CORBIS, p. 38; © Melissa Lockhart/SuperStock, p. 39; © Yuriko Nakao/Reuters/Corbis, p. 41; © Peter M. Wilson/CORBIS, p. 42; © Ken Straiton/Corbis, p. 43. Illustrations by © Bill Hauser/Independent Picture Service.

Front cover: © Steve Vidler/SuperStock.